Stress Solutions

by
Lawrence Vijay Girard

FruitgardenPublishing
"Information and Inspiration
for Living in Harmony with Life"

First Printing 2011

ISBN-10: 0964645793
ISBN-13: 9780964645790

In service to you the reader.
May your life be benefited by
this humble offering.

Contents

Introduction

Many people think that stress is symptomatic of only our modern times. They think that if we could just go back to a simpler time everything would be easy and stress free. Let's take a little journey into the past and see if that is actually true.

Imagine yourself living in a cave and going down to the local watering hole for a cool dip on a hot afternoon. On the way you have to climb a tree and wait for a few minutes while a pack of wild boars go by. Once you get on your way again you get distracted by the noise of an unseen animal thrashing through the bushes to your left, which causes you to take your eyes off the game trail that you are on, and you unintentionally step into something wet, squishy and smelly…oh yes, you are barefoot…shoes won't arrive for about 10,000 years. No problem, this has happened before.

The watering hole is close now; you can just wash your foot when you get there. Oh wait, what is that sound? Oh, it is only a tyrannosaurus! It is a good thing that you smell like poop instead of dinner. Maybe a cool dip isn't such a good idea right now. That might be stressful!

Too far back you say?

Well, how about living in the chaos of ancient Rome. Or maybe you would like to be a Lord or Lady of the middle ages, where starvation and pestilence were lurking in the dark? How about being a slave or having your village plundered? Prefer the old west? That sounds good if you like no indoor plumbing, hauling your water from the well and fear of crop failure.

The truth is that there is no time in history when life has been without challenge. And challenge equals potential for stress: physical, mental and spiritual. It isn't when we live, but how we live, that determines our experience of wellbeing.

We should be the happiest people in the world! We have supermarkets, mobile phones, personal transportation, soft beds, air conditioning, fast food and television; we even have an ambulance that will come and get us if we need help. Yet every one of these comforts has also been a source of stress at one time or another. You say, "How could a soft bed be a source of stress?" Well, if you have ever had a mattress that was too soft and saggy, it probably caused you at least physical and mental stress. And if you use it long enough it may reach all the way into your spirit as well.

Even in the best of times people are faced with birth, death, illness, accidents, relationships, natural disasters and the question of life's purpose. The very nature of life on planet earth is that each day will bring unexpected changes. And change is always fraught with the potential to cause stress.

Introduction

Thus, we can conclude that life equals stress? Well, not exactly. We can say that life equals stress and/or the potential for stress. What's the difference? In nature, we recognize that there are environmental factors that present to everyone, yet everyone doesn't respond to those influences in the same way: this is true mentally, physically and spiritually for all of us.

Our physical genetics and the general condition of our health will affect how we react to our physical environment. Our mental/emotional makeup will determine how we handle things mentally, which will also affect our physical reaction and our spiritual reaction. And of course the state of our spirit will affect our body and mind as well. It is the current state of the body, mind, and spirit that will determine how we react consciously or unconsciously to the challenges of daily life.

The key here is to realize that we can act consciously in life to improve our reaction to influences that we can't always control, while we apply effort to improving things that we can control.

Is stress always bad?

Paul J. Rosch, M.D., M.A., F.A.C.P., the president of the American Institute of Stress has stated, "Increased stress increases productivity - up to a point, after which things rapidly deteriorate, and that level also differs for each of us. It's much like the stress or tension on a violin string. Not enough produces a dull raspy sound and too much an irritating screech or snaps the string – but just the correct degree of stress creates a beautiful tone.

Similarly, we all have to find the right amount of stress that permits us to make pleasant music in our daily lives. You can learn how to utilize and transform stress so that it will make you more productive and less self-destructive."

When we use the stress of life challenges to create positive change in our lives we call it motivation. If those challenges drag us down we call it stress. It is like living in New York City. Some people feel that the hustle bustle is exciting and motivating. While others feel that it is stressful and debilitating. To this we must add the fact that even amongst those who like the stimulation of city life, there is a price to pay. If you like to have a sip of wine once in a while it is not a big thing, but if you become an alcoholic it will be detrimental to your health no matter what you think about it. It is the same when we expose ourselves to continuously stressful environments. If we overdo it, there will be consequences. Yes, you can alleviate many of the symptoms, but you can't cure yourself until you deal with the most systemic issues.

Am I suggesting that moving out of the city is a cure all? No, it is just that we need to see the issues clearly before we can make conscious decisions about how to live in the most beneficial way. Look at people who smoke cigarettes. They know that smoking will eventually kill them if something else doesn't do it first. But they smoke anyway. They have made a choice. What I suggest is that we all make a conscious choice about how we want to deal with the stresses in our lives. Do we want to let stress run wild through our lives like a pack of hyenas? Or do we want to improve the quality of our lives through a conscious act of will. The choice is ours.

In the following chapters we are going to explore some ideas that will be familiar and some that will be new to you. It is common for people to be skeptical of new ideas. I actually encourage fair minded skepticism, as long as it doesn't get in the way of your willingness to explore the unfamiliar in a search for that which is true in life. In fact, this is the basis of the scientific approach to life.

Many of us grew up being told to believe without question what our elders believed. In this day of information availability we now realize that everything our elders taught us was not actually true. If we assume they were sincere in their efforts we can surmise that belief in an idea isn't sufficient in life. We must put our ideas to the test. Experience is the ultimate verification of that which we believe: do our beliefs actually work. And this is what I encourage you to do with these ideas on how to manage the stress in your life. It is only through your own personal experimentation and implementation of these precepts and techniques that you will actually find out if they are true.

"Most folks are about as happy
as they make up their minds to be."
- Abraham Lincoln

"The time is always right
to do what is right."
- Martin Luther King Jr.

"I learned this, at least, by my experiment;
that if one advances confidently
in the direction of his dreams,
and endeavors to live the life which he has imagined,
he will meet with a success
unexpected in common hours."
- Henry David Thoreau

Chapter 1

Time

What time is it? Que hora es? Kitna baghe hey? It doesn't matter if you are asking in English, Spanish or Hindi. What time is it? This is a universal question that has been asked countless times since time immemorial. It doesn't matter if you are a fisherman floating in a canoe down a river looking at the angle of the sun to determine how much time you have left to find a meal, or a Wall Street money broker checking your golden Rolex to see how much time you have before your next big deal, it all amounts to the same thing: time.

Where has the time gone? What time will we get there? How much time will it take? Is it time to go? Do I have enough time? What has happened to the time? Can we make time? Is this the right time? Is this the wrong time? Is there a right time? Yes, it is just a question of time.

Our perception of time in a wide variety of ways can cause us stress. But the simple truth is that time, like the rest of life, is what we make of it. The clock of life can cause us stress if we let it control us or it can relieve us of stress if we use it to our advantage. We need to remember that time is all about what we do with it; what choices we make, in terms of both what we do and how we feel. And in terms of this book, now is the time to share some bad news.

I apologize for starting with bad news, but the expression "I don't have the time!" which is one of the most common responses to the challenge of any kind of self-improvement, doesn't hold water. In fact, it is a bold faced lie that we tell to ourselves while patting ourselves on the back for being so busy.

What do I have in my back pocket to support this bold statement?

Let me ask a question. Do you have time to get sick? You might say no, but if you did get seriously sick or have an accident I assure you, you would take the time to deal with it no matter what was happening in your life: you would have no choice. If any of your loved ones was seriously injured you would drop what you are doing and go to them. The simple truth is that we always have time for the things that are most important to us.

What many people don't consider is that preventive maintenance actually saves time. Just like with a car engine, the time that is taken to properly maintain the motor is much less than the time it takes to repair the motor. It is also less expensive and less stressful!

It is no secret that stress can lead to poor health and diminished mental and physical performance. It can even be a factor in heart attacks and cancer - which can lead to death. Here are some common symptoms of stress:

Common Physical Symptoms include:

Headache
Muscle tension or pain
Chest pain
Fatigue
Change in sex drive
Stomach upset/ulcers
Sleep problems
Weakening of the immune system

Common Mental Symptoms include:

Anxiety
Restlessness
Lack of motivation or focus
Irritability or anger
Sadness or depression
Fear

Common Behavioral Symptoms include:

Overeating or under eating
Anger outbursts
Drug or alcohol abuse
Tobacco use
Social withdrawal

Common Spiritual Symptoms include:

Loneliness
Lack of peace
Lack of joy
Hopelessness
Loss of faith

Stress Solutions

When we say that we don't have time to manage our stress, we are actually saying that we do have time to deal with these symptoms of stress. It just makes practical sense that we should head such problems off at the pass, before they force us off the road and into the bed of illness, anxiety and depression.

Now for the good news!

If we make the choice to improve our lives now, it will help us to avoid future problems and allow us to do so in our own time and way, rather than being forced under more difficult circumstances to do so because of additional stressful consequences. We will also be able to enjoy the benefits of a happier, healthier life. Isn't that worthwhile, instead of seeing this whole subject as a negative?

The next most popular excuse for lack of self-improvement effort is procrastination. "I will do it later. Tomorrow! When I have a chance! In the spring! In the fall! When pigs fly!" Procrastination is the path to failure. Failure is the path to more stress. More stress is the path to more stress!

If we don't take the time or make the time, however you prefer to phrase it, it simply won't happen. It is that simple. If we don't make the choice we will either live under unnecessarily difficult circumstances or life will take hold of us through poor health and force us to act.

There is no time like the present. In fact, there is only the present. Tomorrow doesn't arrive until it becomes the present. And we will never manage our stress until we do it in the right here and now.

In fact, this leads us to our first solution. Practice living in the NOW. Many people have the mental practice of worrying about things from the past or what might go wrong in the future. This mental habit causes us to live in a state of worry consciousness. Worry consciousness is like running a low grade fever that you choose to ignore. You can get away with this for a while if you are generally healthy, but over time this way of approaching life will undermine your health.

When we live in the present, we only have to face what is on the plate of our life once. Why would we want to eat the bad meal of stressful situations more than once? And when we worry about things that haven't even happened we are creating our own mental storm when the winds of life aren't even blowing! Make the choice to live in the present. The past is past, and even plans for the future can only be made in the present.

Make a conscious choice to live fully in the present. Let today be the beginning of your path to a happier, healthier you. Your friends and family will thank you too!

"One of the things I learned the hard way
was it does not pay to get discouraged.
Keeping busy and making optimism a
way of life can restore your faith in yourself."
- Lucille Ball

"Even if you're on the right track
you'll get run over if you just sit there."
- Will Rogers

"If you ask what is the single most important key
to longevity, I would have to say it is
avoiding worry, stress and tension.
And if you didn't ask me, I'd still have to say it."
- George F. Burns

Chapter 2

Diet

Diet is certainly a controversial and challenging subject for many people. Who can keep track of all the diet fads that have floated across the bestselling book lists? I am not about to tell you to eat five tons of broccoli every day! Though as an aside, some fresh broccoli or other green vegetable is certainly a good idea...I personally enjoy broccoli...but I digress. Let's see if we can make this simple.

It is easy to imagine what would happen if you put bad fuel into a car engine: it wouldn't work very well. Over time you wouldn't just experience poor performance, but eventually the vehicle would break down. It is the same with the human body. We need to fuel these bodies with foods that are high in nutritive value and low in unnecessary chemicals and additives if we want them to perform well.

There has been a lot of research done on the subject of food and stress, both on the what causes stress side, as well as, the what reduces stress side. It is not my purpose to get technical here, so let's use a basic common sense approach.

We will continue with the car engine analogy. What causes the most harm in an engine? Heat and friction. Heat is caused by the burning of fuel. Friction also causes heat and wears down the engine parts like sandpaper on wood. Friction and heat equal stress on the engine. So if we want to have less stress we want to have less friction and less heat. What can we do? We put oil in the system. The use of oil, along with pure fuel, is the most powerful way to insure your engine lasts long and performs well. Another thing we do with engines when possible is introduce a cooling system; which is an additional way to remove heat.

So how does this translate into what we should or shouldn't eat for best results in our body/mind/spirit?

When we eat we are fueling our bodies for performance, but we are also causing heat and friction. Foods that are high in fat, stimulants, and toxins cause the body excessive wear and will result in stress and eventually early break down. We even call many of these foods "junk" food. There is no secret about how unhealthy they are for us.

It is the same with what we drink. Soft drinks, coffee, caffeinated tea and alcohol all contain elements that provide short term gain with long term losses. If you consider liquids as a part of the cooling system, it is most beneficial to drink a lot of pure water and fresh fruit juices. So what should we be eating?

The first thing to keep in mind is that there is more than one way to eat well. You should take into account your body type and lifestyle. You should also take into account any specific health issues that you have. Consider consulting with a nutritionist or a physician. There are many books on the subject of diet and educating yourself is well worth the effort. The most general common sense approach is to eat more fresh natural foods and avoid foods that are highly processed with artificial additives, unnecessary chemicals, salt, sugar, preservatives and excessive fat. That might sound like a difficult task considering the plethora of packaged and processed foods that you find into today's supermarkets, but I assure you, if look around you will find plenty of good tasting food that is also good for you.

In recent years vegetarianism has become more and more popular. There are many reasons for this, but here are a few of the main reasons. Scientific research has shown that it is simply not true that meat is an essential part of a healthy diet. Most of us were raised with the misinformation that meat is essential. This is a case of that which was considered common knowledge in the past, has been found to be untrue. It has been found that there are many non meat sources of protein that do not have meat's downside of being hard on the body to digest and full of excessive toxins. From an ecological point of view, it has been determined that it costs more and utilizes more natural resources to raise a cow to eat than it does to grow food that you eat directly. It has also been shown that high red meat consumption can lead to greater risk of many types of cancer.

Some vegetarians claim it is wrong to kill animals to eat them. Interestingly, other vegetarians claim it is wrong to eat animals because they are dead, with no life force, while vegetables, legumes, grains, nuts and fruits are alive with vital life force. Certainly this is a subject for a larger discussion than is appropriate here. I would offer that I personally have been a vegetarian for my whole adult life and have found it to be right for me. I grew up eating meat because that is what was served on the table. At the age of sixteen I learned that I actually had a choice about the matter and after doing my own research on the subject I chose to be vegetarian. I encourage you to explore this subject for yourself so that you can make a conscious choice for your own life.

Most of what I have mentioned so far on diet is within the realm of general common knowledge on the subject. Now I want to share with you a much more subtle aspect to diet. It has to do with the life force and vibrational content of life in general and food in particular. This is an area that has been studied for millennium in the Eastern Cultures, but is relatively new to the Western Culture. Let me start by asking: Who's cooking is best? We all know that it is Mom's cooking that is best. Why would that be so? Along with her cooking being the food you are used to eating, she puts her love into the meal while she cooks. It is Mom's love that is the most powerful part of her good cooking. How and why would that be so?

It was only in the last century that western scientists discovered that this world we live in isn't actually solid. It appears solid to our senses, but it is actually made of energy and lots of space. And in recent years scientists, through the study of Quantum Physics, have discovered that underneath energy, animating all of life, is consciousness. What does this have to do with our diet? Well, just for the same reason that Mom's cooking is best, her consciousness of love has been imbued into the food, so it is that all foods have qualities of consciousness in them. Those energy qualities reflect positive or negative energies that are in life all around us. So if we want to fully understand how we are affected by the food we eat we need to determine what qualities of energy/consciousness are being expressed by the food. This information will help us to determine which foods we want to eat and which we want to avoid.

One of the basic aspects of energy is that it causes the phenomena of magnetism. The more energy present, the more magnetic power is created. We experience this in many ways as we live. We can feel the magnetic presence of people, places, ideas and even food. We have all met people who feel very magnetically appealing or visited a place that just doesn't feel right. We have heard ideas that we inwardly resonate with or reject because of how they feel. It is quite common for children to tell how they feel about food or places very quickly. The ability to inwardly reach out and feel the vibrational essence of life around us is a powerful tool. I have discussed this subject in depth in my book Way of the Positive Flow. For our purpose now, let me share a way to vibrationally evaluate what you eat.

There are three basic categories of life energies: Elevating, Activating and Downward Pulling. Because we are focusing on stress, we will translate those larger concepts into: Stress Reducing, Moderate and Stress Increasing. In this chapter we will apply these categories to food and in the next chapter we will apply them to all of life.

The Three Qualities as applied to food are:

Stress Solutions

Stress Reducing Qualities: Vital with life force, pleasant smell, appealing looks, strong with nutrients, uncooked or lightly cooked, fresh, natural, good tasting without excessive spicing, cooling to the system and the body feels light after eating. Eaten in a quiet, calming environment in silence or friendly conversation with medium sized bites, and chewed well at a leisurely pace with appreciation and moderation. The food cooked in a clean kitchen by attentive people who calmly love and joyfully care about what they are doing.

Stressing Increasing Qualities: No life force, bad smelling, unappealing looks, low nutritive value, hard to digest, over cooked, spoiled, sitting too long in storage, too many spices, filled with unnecessary chemicals and/or toxins, over processed, bad tasting and body feels heavy after eating. Eaten in a noisy, restless and/or angry environment, with loud music and lots of distractions, while taking big bites and swallowing quickly with not enough chewing and/or with a greedy attitude. The food cooked by uncaring people who have a negative attitude in a dirty and noisy environment.

Moderate Qualities: Moderate foods are in the middle between beneficial and not beneficial, so they can go in either a beneficial or not beneficial direction. Canned or frozen vegetables would be a good example - not fresh but not spoiled, food a little over cooked, a mixture of fresh and processed foods, bland tasting, filling the gap of hunger but not fully satisfying or causing indigestion. Eaten in an active but not unpleasant environment with absentminded attention and cooked by people who are generally well meaning but restless.

By looking at these qualities we can see that evaluating the whole process of eating and not just the food itself determines how we are affected by our diet. Why do we care about all of this? Because, beneficial foods are Stress Reducing, Not beneficial foods are Stress Increasing, and moderate foods are a mixture of the two.

With these basic guidelines we can begin to evaluate what, when, where and how we eat in a way that is connected to how we experience stress through our diet. These factors have a much more power effect on us then we might think. If you will begin to observe how you feel before, during and after eating in the light of these three qualities of energy you will begin to see your life in a whole new way. Pay attention to the atmosphere during a meal. Become aware of not only the taste of the food, but how your body feels during and after receiving the food. How does your mind feel after eating? Awake or sleepy? Did you eat too much or too little? Did you get indigestion? Do you feel satisfied?

The more foods that you eat from the Stress Reducing category the happier your body and mind will be. A well running body and mind is the best environment for a joyful spirit. So when we consider the area of diet in our lives, we are actually affecting the totality of our being. I encourage you to explore the many aspects of your dietary life in the light of whether it causes stress or relieves stress, and then begin to make conscious choices that will bring about a calmer, happier and healthier you.

"The way you think, the way you behave,
the way you eat, can influence your life
by 30 to 50 years."
- Dr. Deepak Chopra

"Eating everything you want is not that much fun.
When you live a life with no boundaries,
there's less joy. If you can eat anything you want to,
what's the fun in eating anything you want to?
- Tom Hanks

"The rest of the world lives to eat, while I eat to live."
- Socrates

Chapter 3

Garbage In, Garbage Out

Garbage In, Garbage Out, is a well known saying from the early days of computing. Computer programmers quickly realized that the results that were generated by complicated software programs were only as good as the quality of the inputted information. In other words, you can't make lemonade with prunes. In the last chapter we explored qualities of energy and consciousness in relationship to our diet. Now we are going to expand that concept to the whole of our lives. We need to know how we are experiencing stress in order to discover ways to avoid, reduce or release that stress. The idea that we want to look at everything in life and not just a few obvious areas is key to having the most number of options for creating the best results; which means we are going to work on a systemic level and not just put a band aid on a few problematic symptoms. This might seem like a big project, but it is actually quite simple once you get the hang of it.

What we want to do is use the three qualities: Stress Reducing, Moderate and Stress Increasing as a compass for guiding our lives toward the most beneficial course. We won't be able to create a perfect world on the outside, but we can begin to control our inner weather, how we feel and react to things that stress us. The first step is to become aware of life. Be more conscious about what is going on in life around us and how we are affected by everything we do, everywhere we go, everyone we interact with, and over time we will begin to observe things that we didn't see before. Like many holes that allow the water of our peace to leak from the bucket of our consciousness, we will gradually be able to plug those holes and experience the natural peace of the soul.

Just in the same way that food has an effect on our body/mind/spirit's stress levels, so does everything else in life. When we are exposed to the negative/agitating energies of people and places it can be just the same as if we had eaten a negativity candy bar. What we are going to do is learn to come up with ways to combat stressful situations in the field, as well as, things to do when we get home and have a chance to shower off the grime of stress.

When we live in the Moderate Qualities most of the time, you could say that we are following the path of moderation. This isn't the most elevating way to live, but it is a practical way to live for most people. Then if we apply Stress Reducing influences to counterbalance occasional Stress Increasing influences we will experience general balance.

While this view makes logical sense, it doesn't fully take into account the volume of stressing influences that most people experience each day that are not under our control. So as a practical matter, most of us will need to work hard to increase the Stress Reducing parts of our life to balance out the Moderate and Stress Increasing influences. Only you can decide what you want your life to look like. Just keep in mind that the more time we spend in Stress Reducing influences the happier we will be in body, mind and spirit.

Let's take a look at the three basic qualities as they are applied to our lives in general. Keep in mind that most activities are a mixture of these three qualities and some activities are Stress Reducing when done moderately and Stress Increasing when done to the extreme. For example: Taking a hike in the mountains if you are in good shape can be Stress Reducing. If you are not in good shape it can be Stress Increasing. If you hike up to the top of Mt. Everest it will be physically and mentally stressing but potentially spiritually uplifting. If you get lost on a hike it will be Stress Increasing, but when everything turns out okay and you laugh about it later, it will be Stress Reducing. As you can see, it is the nature of life to be constantly vacillating between the two; there really isn't any rest point in outward life. We are either filling the tank of peace, or it is leaking out through the holes of things that stress us.

In order to get a feel for what we are talking about, let's look at some common activities and see where they fit on the scale of Stress Reducing or Stress Increasing.

Stress Reducing Activities:

Doing things we love to do at moderate levels
Calming activities
Soothing music
Silence
Laughter that is not associated with negative humor

Stress Solutions

Moderate exercise
Reading a good book
Doing art
Hobbies
Writing
Pleasant conversation
Uplifting music
Yoga
Meditation
Enjoying a pleasant wholesome meal
Good friends
Sharing your burdens with a friend/counselor
Conscious breathing
Massage
Living in the now
Immersion in water
Working in the garden
Playing an instrument
Spending time in nature
Hugging your child

Stress Increasing Activities:

Doing any activity that pushes our physical and mental abilities to their limits

Working too hard, for too long, under too much pressure, with unpleasant people

Sitting at a desk for too long

Arguing

Anger

Poor environment: air pollution, noise pollution, flashing lights, stuffiness

Bad posture
Driving on busy roads
Having an unreliable car
Money worries
Relationship Problems
Gambling
Dishonesty
A lack of spiritual connection to life
Arguing
Angry or agitating music
Drug Abuse
Alcohol Abuse

Moderate Activities:

Going to a wholesome movie

Having a party (I don't mean staying up all night and getting drunk or high!)

Playing a game
Generally pleasant music
Cooking
Gardening
Home improvement projects
Going out to eat
Working at a job under positive conditions
Having a good time with your children
Going on a vacation
A day at the amusement park

Stress Solutions

Watching a reasonable amount of television
Sports

You will note that many of these activities could be in more than one category; it depends on how that activity is engaged in as to the totality of its effect on us. Playing some video games could be a moderate activity, but if you do it for hours it will become a Stress Increasing activity. It would be the same with spending time in the garden. If you are enjoying it then it is Stress Reducing, but if you do it to the point that it becomes a burden, it becomes Stress Increasing. This is why we need to pay attention to life as it presents itself to us and not just statically say, "This is good and that is bad." Life is a flow that we must maneuver through like a canoe going down a river. Sometimes the middle of the river is the best place to be and sometimes closer to the bank is best. Occasionally we will need to negotiate the rapids no matter what part of the river we prefer. We need to stay attentive and flexible. If you are on the river, you will get wet, so don't act surprised!

As a general guideline, it is Stress Reducing to simplify our lives. Many people make their lives unnecessarily complicated - which is Stress Increasing - and then think that the load they carry in life is normal and necessary. Take the time to honestly evaluate your life. Since we are often too close to our own lives to see them clearly, consider getting help in this process from a friend and/or mentor. Look at how you are affected by everything you do and make changes in the light of what we have been discussing. If you experiment with these ideas you will find that they can have a powerful beneficial effect on reducing the level of stress in your life.

Chapter 4

Exercise

The old adage "Use it or lose it!" pretty much says what we need to hear. You wouldn't think that under using your body would be Stress Increasing, but it is. There have been plenty of people who have experimented with planting themselves on the couch in order to combat stress. And certainly there is a time and place for couch surfing, especially if your job already provides you with lots of exercise, but just using the body's muscles alone isn't the main point here. We also want to explore how energy flowing through the body affects the mind and spirit as well.

There are three kinds of tension that we experience in life: Physical, Mental and Spiritual. It is essential to understand that they are inter-related. Mental tension can cause physical tension, which can cause spiritual tension. Spiritual tension can cause mental and then physical tension. Life is a totality, not just its individual components. Here are some of the ways we create tension in our lives:

Physical Tension Causes

Insufficient physical activity
Unhealthy Food and/or eating habits
Excessive repetitive motions
Illness
Injury
Improper posture
Improper lifting
Poor mattress
Mental Stress
Excessive exercise
Poor thinking habits

Mental Tension Causes

Job
Relationships
Money
Too many things to do
Illness or feeling run down
Loneliness
Fears
Worries
Success and/or Failure
Opinion of self
Mental approach to life

Spiritual Tension Causes

Low self-esteem
Lack of life purpose
Loneliness
Lack of peace
Lack of joy
Lack of faith

Lack of belonging
Lack of friendship
Lack of love
Hopelessness
No belief in a higher power or order (not necessarily religion)

So how can exercise help us deal with these tensions? Through exercise we become stronger. When we are strong, we are able to comfortably ignore many of life's little irritants. A mosquito trying to bite the back of a crocodile doesn't have much of an effect. When we are physically, mentally and spiritually strong there isn't much in life that can hurt us.

Exercise is also a form a cleansing; it allows the body to release tensions and toxins by getting the blood flowing vigorously through all of the body parts. This works for the mind as well when you are doing the right form of exercise for you. If you are thinking of your problems while you exercise, you aren't getting the full benefit of your efforts. Try to exercise in a way that also occupies your mind in a positive way. If your type of exercise is something that you really enjoy doing, all the better; that means your spirit will be improved as well.

Let's take a closer look at how this works. When we are exercising at something we enjoy doing, energy and enthusiasm are flowing through us. Since our energy is flowing towards our positive purpose of exercise, it isn't going towards other areas of life. So at minimum we are getting a vacation from our problems. Over time we will find that many of life's tensions can be released through a good workout. And sometimes, just by getting your mind off your problems for a while, you will relax enough so that a solution to one of your challenges, instead of having to fight its way through your mental struggle, will easily be able to present itself to your mind.

When we don't feel burdened by life's ups and downs it is much easier for the soul's natural level of joy and wellbeing to emerge. Regardless of your spiritual beliefs, or lack thereof, physical accomplishment leads to physical health and mental wellbeing - which are beneficial parts of spiritual wellbeing.

You don't need to be an Olympic athlete to be healthy. But it is good to challenge yourself. So experiment with different ways you can have fun and get healthy. You don't have to do just one thing: cross training is great. Be sure to take into account your general health and age. And don't overdo it on the first day! Many an exercise plan was defeated in the first week due to muscle soreness from over enthusiasm.

Exercise Suggestions for Experimentation

Join a gym
Join a coed softball, volleyball or bowling league
Take a walk
Jog
Ride a horse
Ballroom dancing
Ride a bicycle
Hiking and trekking
Take up any sport that interests you
Swimming
Martial Arts
Yoga

Exercise

I saved Yoga for last on the list because it holds a special place in terms of exercising for the release of stress. The science of yoga was developed thousands of years ago in India. Its purpose was to explore life from the inside out, through the inner self, rather than the outside in, the way Western scientists approach the exploration of life.

The yoga teachings include much more than the practice of Yoga Postures or Asana, which is the best known part of yoga in the West. Meditation techniques are also a part of the yoga teachings and we will discuss them in chapter eight. Yoga Posture exercises were originally designed not so much for health, but as preparation for meditation. In order to meditate well the body must be held erect without tension. So the Yoga Postures have as their main purpose the releasing of tension from both the body and the mind.

Let me share with you a couple of simple exercises that you can try, so that you can see how effective these exercises can be for releasing stress. As you do the exercises, do not injure yourself! Take into account your current physical condition and only do what feels safe and comfortable. If you ever feel lightheaded during the exercise, stop and sit down.

Full Yogic Breath

1.   Stand in a comfortable upright position. Take a mental inventory of how you feel.
2.   Bending at the waist, lean forward and relax down until your hands are as close to touching the floor as they can comfortably be. Do not force your hands lower, just relax.

3.   Now, using the palms of the hands, sweep your hands up the body - keeping the palms about 8 inches from the skin. While you sweep the hands upward inhale slowly and deeply through the nose.

4.   When you get to the top reach your hands up until they are extended as far as you can above the head and hold for just a moment.

5.   Now, again using the palms to sweep in front of the body, go down, exhaling slowly through the mouth. Pace yourself according to your breathing capacity.

6.   Once you get to the bottom, go up again inhaling and then down exhaling, repeat for a total of three times.

7.   End after your last extension of hands towards the sky. Exhale while you keep the body upright and bring the hands gracefully to the sides.

8.   Breathe normally and take a mental inventory. How do you feel now?

If you did this exercise, you will now feel more aware of how you feel, and you will also feel mentally calmer. Your body should also feel just a little bit more relaxed.

Deep Relaxation

1.   Lay down comfortably on your back. It can be on the floor or on your bed.

2.   Inhale through the nose with a short and then a long inhalation. The inhalation is: In Innnnnn. As you inhale, try to tense all of the muscles in the body - tense low, medium, high in a flow - at the same time. This will take some practice. So you are inhaling with a double breath while you tense all of the muscles.

3.   Hold the breath with muscles at high tension for the count of three.

4. Exhale with a double breath out the mouth. The exhalation is: Out Ouuuuuuut. While you relax the muscles in a flow – high, medium, low, relaxed.

5. Repeat the double breath with tension two more times, being sure to tense and relax the muscles in a flow and completely relax at the end of the exhalation.

6. After the third repetition get comfortable and then hold the body absolutely still. Do not move a muscle.

7. We are now going to turn off the energy to the muscles in the body. Starting with your feet, mentally shut off the energy to your feet. Feel that they are dissolving away. And then go up the body doing the same relaxing and dissolving process to every part of the body. The calves, the thighs, the buttocks, the abdomen, the chest and back, the arms, the shoulders, the neck and the head.

8. Stay absolutely still with the energy switched off to all the body parts for several minutes. You may fall asleep, that's okay.

9. After some time, when you choose to, you should gently turn the energy on again by lightly wiggling the toes. And then rocking the head slowly side to side.

10. When you are ready, sit up and mentally take inventory of how you feel. You should feel more relaxed physically and mentally.

This is just a little taste of what Yoga Postures can do to help you release stress. I should mention that there are many different styles of Yoga Postures being taught around the world today. You will need to do some research in your area to see what is offered and then try some different classes to see which is best for you. Include in your evaluations not only the exercises, but the style of the instructor and the feeling of the classroom environment.

Stress Solutions

I encourage you to explore the Ananda Yoga style of postures if it is available in your area. It focuses more on relaxation and less on the athletic side of the exercises than most other styles. You can find more information about Ananda Yoga at: www.AnandaYoga.Org. But, as I mentioned, almost any style will get you going in a beneficial direction.

As you explore different ways to get your body moving don't forget to exercise your spirit. When possible, exercise in nature. Hiking in the foothills is much better than walking a treadmill. Surfing, skiing, biking and various other sports will get you out in fresh air and allow your spirit to commune with nature's essential healing powers. Try it if you aren't already doing it. You might like it!

Chapter 5

Hobbies/Recreation

In the last chapter we focused on exercising the body. In this chapter we are going to focus on exercising the mind and the use of our creative potential. Possibly you have found a way to make a living doing what you love most. If you have, I congratulate you! And I encourage those who haven't yet found a way to make a living doing what you love most, don't give up the dream. At the same time, sometimes when we make a job out of our hobby, it doesn't feel like a hobby any more. So keep that in mind as well.

How we feel about what we are doing in life has a big impact on the totality of our lives. If we hate what we are doing on a day to day basis, it will infect our peace, our health and our relationships. Having a hobby that you do just for the love of doing it can be a great way to release stress that builds up in your life no matter where it comes from.

It really doesn't matter what you do. It can be more recreational like fishing, boating, camping, and four wheeling, or it can be stamp collecting, model building or leading a Cub Scout troop. And you don't have to have just one! You can mix and match any way you like. No matter what you choose to do there are a few important features that you should keep in mind.

I love it!

Your hobby should be something that you really enjoy doing. You should experience a positive feeling of anticipation towards this activity. If you don't feel that, then consider looking for an additional activity that does bring that feeling. When you feel enthusiasm for something you love flowing through your consciousness, it means positive energies are both distracting you from your problems and clearing out the negative energies associated with those problems. It is like taking a cooling dip in a pool on a hot day. There is a relaxing of body, mind and spirit. This is definitely Stress Reducing, and you aren't even doing it yet!

Fully Engaging

Your hobby should be, as much as possible, fully engaging to your body, mind and spirit. When you are participating you should be so absorbed in the activity that you do not think of other things. Or at least, none of the things you think about should be connected to your life challenges. This is vacation time and you don't want thoughts of other activities to pollute the clear waters of your revitalization.

Experience Wellbeing

You should experience a feeling of wellbeing when you are engaged in your hobby. This is different than a rush of fun and excitement. It is a feeling of contentment. While excitement may be a component of your hobby, it shouldn't be the main reason for your participation. Excitement of the emotions is always followed at some point by an emotional letdown. This up and down emotional rollercoaster approach to life is very Stress Increasing. When we feel the peace that is associated with our spirit, it will be like an artesian spring of peace or joy. This upward bubbling of good feeling has no corresponding negative emotion.

Creative thinking

While it is nice at times to have a hobby that allows you not to think hard, it is helpful if one of your hobbies includes the need for creative thinking and/or problem solving. Many people think that relaxation comes from doing little or nothing. And certainly there is a time and place for resting the body and mind in that way. But when we open our minds up to our creative potential we begin to tap resources that are greater than our own. In this process we free ourselves from the limits of logic and explore the potentials of intuitive perception.

Intuition is like using the wind to power a boat. The wind is blowing whether you use it or not. Creative potential is always present. We need to raise the sail of our mental interest to capture the wind of inspiration. And in the same way you adjust a sail to best capture the wind, we must learn to attune our minds to creative potential in order to draw the most out of that potential. When we use our hobby to develop ourselves in this way, we will enjoy more and accomplish more, while at the same time feeling invigorated instead of tired. Once we get the hang of it we will find this process spilling over to benefit the rest of life as well.

Service to Others

When possible, include service to others in this part of your life. Conscious service to others, regardless of how they receive our service, is a very powerful force for good in our own consciousness. When we are concerned for the welfare of others we begin to break the chain that holds many of our perceived problems to us. Problems in life are like someone ringing the doorbell. If you are too busy helping others to answer, many of those problems will stop ringing in your mind. Surprisingly, many problems in life that seem to be calling to us with the loudest voice will magically disappear if you just ignore them. Problems that don't go away through neglect won't seem so big when we put them into the larger perspective of some of the problems that others have in this life. I am not suggesting that we ignore the practical side of health, financial or other problems, I am just pointing out that many of life's little irritants will go away if we don't keep scratching at them.

Ultimately we want to see most of life as service to others, even when we are being paid. When we live in the consciousness of service we will experience more and more of the joy of the soul instead of living for the gaining of outward comfort or reward, which will never in itself lead to happiness.

Service can be done in many ways. You could volunteer at a nonprofit group. You could coach a youth sports team or participate in scouting. You could visit sick children in a hospital. You could teach a class in your area of interest. Today people even take service vacations, where they go to a foreign country and do a service project. The ideas are endless. The main thing here is to include others in your circle of caring and you will find that through less concern for yourself you will experience less stress.

Leave your hobby with a smile.

When you are done with your hobby for the day, you should be excited about doing it again as soon as possible. If you do it for too long it may leave a bad taste in our mouth. Overextending ourselves even in things that we enjoy is Stress Increasing. When you finish while wishing you could stay longer, you will carry positive anticipation towards next time. Learning to live with positive anticipation is Stress Reducing. This doesn't mean that we should live in the future. It means that we should carry a calm feeling of life's positive potential with us all the time. This positive attitude will protect us from many of the Stress Increasing arrows that life shoots at us.

Just in the same way that physical exercise works out the kinks in your body, your hobby will help work out the kinks in your mind. The positive enthusiastic energy that flows through your consciousness while you are engaged in your hobby will sweep away the clutter of many tensions. It will distract you from many problems so that you will feel recharged when you are once again ready to face those challenges. You may also find, just as with exercise, that a mental vacation from your stresses gives your mind time to assimilate your life challenges and then, seemingly out of nowhere, a new solution may present itself.

"Creative minds have always been known
to survive any kind of bad training."
- Anna Freud

"Where the spirit does not work
with the hand there is no art"
- Leonardo da Vinci

"The creative is the place where no one else has ever been.
You have to leave the city of your comfort and go into the
wilderness of your intuition. What you'll discover will be
wonderful. What you'll discover is yourself."
- Alan Alda

Chapter 6

Relationships

No matter what goes wrong in life, when people are forced through circumstances beyond their control to be reminded of that which is most important: Spirit, family, friends, community and country come first. When the relationships in these parts of our life are well tended, we will have minimized the chances that the weeds of stress will overcome us.

Spirit

No matter how you define your spiritual view of life, or lack of a spiritual view, the reality is that we must individually come to grips with this part of life if we want to be at peace. If you follow a religion or spiritual practices that fulfill you, then you know how powerful this part of life can be. If you aren't active in your spiritual life, I encourage you to try and figure out why. No matter what path you follow, the key is participation. When we feel a positive connection to life's greater realities then life's ups and downs don't feel so stressful.

Stress Solutions

If you don't have any particular spiritual path or even if you are an atheist, I encourage you to think outside of the box of preconception. Many people discount the possibility of a greater or divine reality because of the countless mistakes that have been done throughout the centuries by people who claim to represent God. We know even in the most simple of circumstances in life that people often, for both noble and ignoble reasons, misrepresent the truth. The only way to know for sure is to go directly to the source. I encourage you to inwardly challenge God/Nature/the Universe to have a dialogue with you. Inwardly ask your questions and see of life doesn't in some inward or outward way respond. Don't expect a voice in the clouds – though I suppose it could happen. It is more likely that you will meet someone, or find a book or have some other experience that will subtly guide you in a new positive direction. Of course, don't ask if you don't really want to know!

Friendship

Friendship is at the center of the very best relationships. This is the open hearted giving and receiving of love and concern. While it is common to have a best friend, the spirit of friendship is one that we should bring to all relationships. This positive approach to life allows good feelings to flow through our consciousness: which is Stress Reducing and joy increasing. When we hold everyone off at a distance we are building a wall around ourselves: which is Stress Increasing and joy reducing.

Be a friend to all and you will find that you live in a world of friends. If others close you off because they don't want to be friends, then accept their decision out of respect for their right to do so. That doesn't mean you can't still be their friend. Possibly over time, through your positive attitude, they will change their minds. History has shown us that many people who started as enemies, over time became the best of friends. When we keep the positive attitudes of friendship in our hearts, we will feel the Stress Reducing benefits of that energy no matter what others decide to do.

Spouse

Our relationship with our spouse or significant other is a barometer of how our life is going. When this most personal relationship is not going well it stresses us to the core. When we are in harmony at home, we are more able to deflect many of life's stresses. It is quite common for couples to take this relationship for granted and not give it the regular appreciation and nurturing that it needs and deserves. Investing your time and energy in this relationship is Stress Reducing. Letting this relationship die through neglect is Stress Increasing.

Children

The relationship between child and parent is one of the most beautiful expressions of life. At the same time, this relationship can be the most challenging and stressful of all. The sheer volume of attention and energy that childrearing involves should give us a hint that we are going to be worn out. But, as we have all experienced, there is pleasant worn out and unpleasant - Stress Increasing - worn out.

I have often wondered why we don't think twice about taking a course and/or reading a book to increase our ability to succeed in business or a hobby, but we don't always consider doing the same for raising our children. Most parents just wander down the path of life trusting that their instincts or the way that they were raised will be sufficient for the task. Well certainly we can see that most people survive childhood, so in the most basic way that approach does work. But, if we want to reduce stress in our lives, there may be a better way. Good preparation for any life challenge is Stress Reducing. I encourage you to explore ideas about how to raise your children in the most effective way with the least amount of stress.

As it happens…err…um…I have written a book called Positive Flow Parenting. In this book I point out that it is, who we are as people, that will determine the most important part of how we parent. Taking control of our lives and living with less stress consciousness will of its own accord be beneficial to this most special part of life.

Family

We usually think of family as our relatives by blood and/or through marriage. But there are other ways to experience family as well. Soldiers often feel this close bond with their comrades in arms. People on teams of all kinds can feel a sense of family. Even hobby enthusiasts of many kinds feel a sense of family with others of the same interests. All of the types of families express the value of belonging. When we feel that we belong we are happier and happy feelings mean less stress. No matter the type of family that draws you, be it a spiritual family, a recreation family or a blood relations family, spending time with your family will be Stress Reducing.

Business

In business we relate to our colleagues, vendors and customers. All of these relationships hold the potential for stress. At the same time, all of these relationships also hold the potential to be Stress Reducing. The most powerful determining factor in which way these relationships will turn is in us. When we bring the spirit of friendship and family to our business life, we will be happier no matter what happens. And if we bring an adversarial attitude to these relationships we will live in that negative energy, which will have a Stress Increasing effect on us.

People who believe that they can be ruthless in business and be unaffected inwardly don't take into account how life actually works. We often see in movies how the hero goes around punching people in order to save the day. What you don't usually see portrayed is that using your fist to hit someone most commonly hurts your fist as well. There is always a price to pay when we put out any kind of negative energy. We all know the saying "What goes around, comes around." This is a practical truth about how life works no matter what our beliefs may be. Positive business relationships are Stress Reducing and negative business relationships are Stress Increasing.

Community

When we care about our community we expand our sense of self. This expansion takes us out of preoccupation with or own needs -Stress Increasing - and allows us to be concerned with the needs of others - Stress Reducing. Of course if we over personalize the challenges of others then they can become Stress Increasing. What we want to do is try to make the world a better place while realizing that it isn't ours to solve every problem.

Take the time to care about your community. Do what you can, in the ways that work for you, to make your community a better place. No matter how much or how little your efforts seem to be, they will be a positive - Stress Reducing - influence on your own life.

Country

Allegiance to one's country can be challenging at times. When we see politicians saying and doing the same old thing year after year, while they act like they are breaking new ground, it can be downright Stress Increasing. At the same time, believing in the best of your country and doing what you can to improve things is living for a noble cause. When we live connected to a purpose that is higher than our own needs, we are tapping into a powerful force for the experience of wellbeing. Many people have given their lives, with peace in their hearts, when they gave the ultimate sacrifice for a noble cause. We shouldn't discount the Stress Reducing potential of attunement to a noble cause. Explore your own life opportunities to be part of something noble and you will find this out for yourself.

The World

Think globally, act locally, is a well known slogan for the ecology movement. I encourage you to consider bringing this concept into all areas of life. Through the power of global communications the world has never been more aware of not only the family of humanity, but the family of all life. Our planet is one biosphere and the lives of all living things are connected. This global perception can be used as a pathway to greater peace and cooperation. It is our responsibility to participate in the process of bringing peace to the world, by bringing peace into our own lives, and then expanding that peace in every way we can. Living consciously as a channel for peace in life is Stress Reducing.

When we take the time to give these areas of life the attention they deserve we are investing in the wellbeing of all. That is one of the most powerful truths of life, that when we act in the best ways it isn't only for ourselves. Everyone benefits when we live in the best possible way.

"We are not human beings on a spiritual journey.
We are spiritual beings on a human journey."
- Stephen R. Covey

"Rejoice with your family in the beautiful land of life!"
- Albert Einstein

"You don't choose your family.
They are God's gift to you, as you are to them."
- Desmond Tutu

Chapter 7

Controlling Your Inner Weather

Taking life's ever-new nature into account is essential. This is why lists of do's and don'ts, don't actually work. We need an approach to life that takes into account our individual nature and circumstances. Keep in mind that change in life is directional from where we are now. What we want to do is become clearly aware of our current state of affairs and then nudge our life in a positive direction.

The three part process that we are now going to explore will give us a sense of our current circumstances while providing ideas about how to proceed and a positive approach to working with our experimentations in De-Stressing our lives. Keep in mind that this is an active process that requires three basic steps which will be applied simultaneously once we become proficient in our application. The three components are: Awareness, Inspiration and Application.

Awareness

There are two aspects of awareness. The first is

our perception of our body/mind/spirit. How do I feel? Am I calm or agitated? Am I generally happy or sad? Am I energetic or lethargic? Do I feel satisfied or unfulfilled? These are all questions that help us determine the state of our inner weather. The second aspect of awareness is our perception of life around us. What is going on out there? Not just the conditions themselves, but the qualities of energy underneath those conditions. What we want to do is reach out with our inner awareness, while our senses look and listen, to feel the truth underneath the surface of life.

Through developing our inner awareness of self and life around us we will be able to recognize the presence or absence of stress. In the same way that an eardrum resonates with sound waves to provide the ability to hear, we can learn to perceive how we are inwardly resonating with life around us. Through this inner perception we can more clearly observe what is stressing us and how it is affecting us.

Let's take a walk through the park to see how this works.

As you arrive at the park you may notice that there is a relaxing of the mind as soon as you step into the park. Part of this is due to the positive effect that being in nature has on us. The mind also may remember previous good experiences at the park and open itself up to receiving more of the same. It would be natural to visually and aurally take in your surroundings as you arrive. Is the grass green? Are there kids laughing on the jungle gym? Is that a bird in one of the trees? These are things you might see and hear. Now reach out with your inner awareness to embrace the park. Can you feel the calmer atmosphere of the open space in the park? Do you feel the happy go lucky aura around the children? Are the birds chirping with good cheer? Or is there heaviness in the air? Are the kids yelling with combative aggression? Are the birds squawking with alarm? Is there a parent yelling at their child? These different views of the park can be perceived with both our senses and our inner intuitive sense. We want to practice using both. It is the totality of our inner and outer awareness that will give us the complete picture of what is going on in life.

Next we want to feel how each part of our experience affects our feeling of more or less stress. Kids yelling would probably be Stress Producing. The friendly chirping of birds might be Stress Reducing. The rich green colors of healthy grass, bushes and trees would be Stress Reducing, while almost stepping on dog poop would be Stress Producing. The unexpected loud backfire of a car would be Stress Producing, while the sounds of water in a fountain would be Stress Reducing. And thus like the ocean, the waves of life experiences are always washing up upon the shores of our consciousness and we react to them as Stress Increasing or Stress Reducing.

Through practice you will learn to move through life with your inner awareness activated, just in the same way we are used to living through the senses. This is not ESP or any other kind of occult power. It is to a greater or lesser degree, according to the unique nature of each individual person, a natural ability that comes as standard equipment when we are born. That most of us weren't educated on this subject when we were growing up is not sufficient reason to discount the possibility of this being true. Experiment for yourself and see what happens.

Stress Solutions

Now that you have a sense of what I am talking about, begin to look with your inner perceptions at everything in your life. Through this inner process you will see clearly all of the large and little ways that you feel stressed. This information will be the basis for dealing with stress on both a global, all of your life scale, and on an individual stress by stress scale.

Inspiration

Once we recognize that we are feeling stress and gain greater understanding about where it is coming from, we need to come up with creative ideas about how to avoid stress, release stress, or become so inwardly strong that stress, like a single drop of water entering the ocean, doesn't really affect us. What we want to do is tap our own inner creative potential to come up with ways that work for us, in our own unique situation. Inspiration can come from your own creative center or it can come from friends, counselors, and books, the key is to come up with some ideas and try them out to see what happens.

It has been my personal experience that life itself is my friend. When I need new ideas I just ask God/Life/the Universe. I am not talking about a specific religious belief. If you have one, use it. If you don't, experiment with the idea that life itself will respond when you ask a direct question. Once you have asked the question, use your inner awareness to observe how life responds. An idea might pop into your mind, you might see an article or you might hear the conversation of others that somehow sounds like the answer to your question. I know that this might sound strange to some people, but I can assure you that millions of people throughout history have experienced this to be true. If you are scientifically minded, do the experiment for yourself. And don't pollute the experiment with doubt. Just keep an open mind and see what happens. What can it hurt?

When you practice seeking solutions to life challenges through your inner connection to life you will find that things work out in amazing and wonderful ways. Sometimes you receive ideas about what to do and sometimes life just changes before your eyes and the need for an answer dissipates. One of the most Stress Releasing things you can do is give your problems to God. Through that process you will feel better regardless of what happens with your specific need.

No matter where your inspirations come from, the point is to come up with ideas that you can apply to our next step: Application.

Application

This is where we begin to experiment with the ideas and observations that we come up with about how to improve our lives. Before we explore some examples of how this whole process works, let me share one more tip for improving your chances of success.

I mentioned earlier that life is directional from where we are today. For our current purpose we are focusing on the subject of stress. But in the larger context of all aspects of life, we can generally say that positive energies in life are beneficial and negative energies are not beneficial. Sometimes in order to attain our goals in life we are tempted to block negative energies in some way through the power of our will. Certainly this is necessary on occasion, but for the most part there is a very effective alternative. What we want to do is, instead of standing against or trying to block what we perceive as a negative situation, we want to creatively apply some energy in order to redirect the negative energy into a positive direction rather than going against it.

Here is how this might work.

So you find yourself in a conversation with someone who is complaining to no end. It doesn't matter the subject. The fact is their negative energy is causing you to feel stressed. You may be tempted to tell them to shut up. But that would go against the person's energy and possibly create more tension. So what you do is ask them a question in order to change the subject. If possible, let your question be concerning something about which you know they have positive feelings. With some people you may have to ask several new questions. They may be so negative that everything they talk about is negative. And then you might want to consider removing yourself from the situation. You may ultimately have to tell them to shut up if it seems necessary. But the positive redirection of negative energy is potentially Stress Reducing instead of Stress Increasing.

Sometimes people are super positive but not focused. You can use this same technique with them. Just subtly redirect their energy in a useful way. This can be fun and of great benefit to all.

So now let's put it all together in a number of situations. Just keep in mind that what you want to do is train yourself to come up with your own unique way of using this process.

At Home

Situation: You are having guests over for dinner.

Controlling Your Inner Weather

You got home late from work and you don't have as much time as you expected for preparations. You started feeling stressed when you realized you wouldn't leave the office on time. It got worse when you got in the car and traffic was even slower than usual. Now you are in the kitchen, you are feeling overwhelmed, and you don't know what to do.

Solution 1: Don't let yourself get worked up in the first place. No matter what happens things will work out. If you let yourself get all stressed, it doesn't help anything, it just makes you uncomfortable.

Solution 2: Anticipate that things will go wrong in life. As often as possible, have a backup plan. When your backup plan evaporates....improvise!

Solution 3: Take a deep conscious breath. With the inhalation take in positive calming energy, and with the exhalation release all tension. Now smile and push calmly forward because you just redirected your own energy!

Solution 4: Much more important than the food is the happy greeting that your guests find when they arrive. If they feel your tension, they might become stressed. If you aren't motivated to keep calm for yourself, keep calm for others.

Solution 5: If you don't have time to cook what you planned, make a salad and order out. Or boil some water and make pasta. You can even turn your fancy dinner into a picnic and have everyone make their own sandwiches. Even peanut butter and jelly is better than stress.

Solution 6: The truth will set you free! If folks arrive too soon, tell them what happened, they will understand and probably offer to pitch in and help. Even if you are the greatest cook in the world, your guests are probably more

Stress Solutions

interested in visiting with you than what they actually eat. And don't forget, disasters make the best stories once we have gotten through them, so exchange your feelings of stress for a smile.

At Work

Situation: Your boss is a big SOB but you can't afford to quit your job.

Solution 1: Remember that Rome wasn't built in a day; so pace yourself. When we give others power over our inner peace, it is our fault not theirs. They may give us the motivation to feel tense, but it is our choice as to what actually happens within the realm of our own inner kingdom. So be the Queen/King of your own life and choose peace.

Solution 2: Remember the basic precept that just a little energy applied in the right place can make a big difference. You just need to find the right button to push. Find out if the boss has a hobby and talk about it. Do you have a mutual friend? Do some research and experiment with ideas about how to find common ground.

Solution 3: People who are grumpy and hard to get along with are in pain. It is their own internal war that causes them to be that way. Embrace compassion and see if there is something you can do to help them heal.

Solution 4: No matter how others treat you, keep your dignity. Once they figure out that you can't be inwardly shaken, they will respect you. They still may fire you. But they will respect you!

Solution 5: Be patient. It helps you and it helps others as well. Ask the Universe to present you with a solution. It may take some time, but eventually one will present itself.

In a Restaurant

Situation: Everything is going wrong. The restaurant is too noisy, the service is to slow and the food is overpriced and not very tasty.

Solution 1: When you first arrived did it feel like things were going to go well? When I arrive in a restaurant and it doesn't feel comfortable to me, I turn around and go out. I don't get snippy about it; I just realize that I have come to the wrong place for me. Once I decide to stay, I try to accept what happens with internal grace. If I don't, and I get upset, then I only have myself to blame.

Solution 2: I actually find it entertaining when things go wrong in a restaurant. I am interested to see how the waiter and/or the manager will handle things. When you observe people handling difficult situations well, it is quite inspiring. When I meet people who do their jobs well I look for the opportunity to tell them that I have noticed.

Solution 3: It often occurs to me that life is messing with my head. So when things go wrong I almost always get a smile on my face. Once we see the joke of it we feel better no matter what happens.

Solution 4: Politely offer a workable solution to the situation. Sometimes people get flustered and they don't know what to do, your suggestion might help.

Solution 5: Don't ever go back! Unless of course, you feel mysteriously guided to have more of the same kind of fun.

On the Road

Situation: Everything is going wrong. Someone cut me off. I am getting low on gas. The trip is taking longer than expected. I am hungry but I don't have time to stop for food.

Solution 1: Anticipation. Everything that can go

wrong in life will eventually do so, so why be surprised? Plan for the worst and hope for the best. Don't forget, the worse the situation, the better the story!

Solution 2: I must admit that I have occasionally visualized powering up my laser blasters and zapping a few crazy commuters, like the time I was driving and a guy just sort of drifted over into my lane and I had to swerve to avoid him. Later that same day, my mind was wandering off into what at the time seemed like an important subject, until I got honked on by a guy that was already in the lane that I was starting to pull into. One of the great laws of life is: What goes around comes around. Isn't there a another saying that goes, "Judge not lest ye be judged." I don't care what religion a person does or doesn't follow; I think that saying makes a lot of sense.

Solution 3: Years ago I discovered that some smart person put books on cassette tape. Now they have them on CD's. I get them at the public library, so they don't cost a cent. I have driven many a happy mile while listening to all kinds of books. That sure beats getting all steamed up inside over something that I can't control. This is a case where instead of redirecting other people's energy, I redirect my own energy.

Solution 4: It is always a good idea to keep a little emergency kit in the car. You never know when it might come in handy. If you keep some food and water in the car, it will be there when you need it.

Solution 5: Anticipation! I, like many, have watched the fuel needle in my car tip perilously close to empty while I watched a "Gas in ten miles" sign go by. Who's fault is this? Mine! If this gives me stress who is to blame? I am! Enough said.

With Children

Situation: It is bed time and the kid(s) won't go to sleep.

Solution 1: Anticipation! Make sure your children are mentally and physically prepared to sleep. That means no stimulants like sugar, television, video games and vigorous running around within an hour or more before sleep time. One caveat to the no food rule is that with babies it is helpful to have them hungry and worn out before bedtime. That way they are most likely to fall asleep right after you feed them. And with a full stomach they will be able to sleep longer. It also means there should be no recent naps that would keep them awake.

Solution 2: No one ever said this was going to be easy. Smile!

Solution 3: Training. Regularity increases the chances of acceptance. Create a going to bed routine, the more you use it, the more comfortable your children will be with it.

Solution 4: I encourage you to read to your children. This makes a great way for children to transition into a relaxed state of mind. It is also a great way to share time with your children. As my children got older we would take turns making up the story. In that way they also learned to think creatively.

As you can see, all of these potential solutions lead to you experiencing less stress. They also include concern about the possibility of stressing others. When we include the needs of others along with our own needs we will find that we are creating an atmosphere around our lives that is much less likely to encourage stress.

Stress Solutions

When we become aware of the qualities of energy that are behind all life experiences we can begin to work with the underlying causes of stress instead of just the symptoms. In all of these examples we can see that life isn't so much about what happens, but about how we react to what happens. As I said earlier, being happy in life is all about choice. We do what we can to improve things, but no matter what happens, we always get to choose how we react. When we choose peace, stress won't have a hook on which to hang its hat.

Chapter 8

Meditation

Where can happiness be found? Everyone knows the answer to this question: Within. Yet where do most people look for happiness? Outside of ourselves! So why would we look outside ourselves when we know that happiness is found within? Because one of the unique features of life as we experience it is that we feel compelled, as the result of unseen forces, to believe, in spite of common sense and evidence to the contrary, that we can somehow grasp happiness through an outward experience. As a practical matter, it doesn't really matter why we look outside for happiness, what matters is what we do about it.

Meditation is the science and art of stillness…er…um…I happen to have written a book just on this subject, called *Meditation: The Science and Art of Stillness*. What does stillness have to do with it? Well imagine your mind as an expanse of water. When it is perfectly still it is at peace. When the wind blows or you throw rocks into it then waves are caused which disturb the natural peace of the mind. Meditation is the use of specific techniques that are designed to still the mind from the disturbances of outward life.

The mind gets some relief during sleep. But sleep takes us into the subconscious mind; where we can only get limited relief from stress. Peace, joy and understanding come from the superconscious mind – which is that part of the mind that is also associated with creative inspiration and upliftment. Meditation is the most direct way to calm the mind and experience the most systemic form of stress reduction.

Let's do an experiment.

Step 1 - Take a mental inventory of how you feel right now. You can close your eyes if you want. (But only after you read steps two and three!)

Step 2 - Take a deep breath in the nose. Hold for the count of three. Exhale through the mouth. Do this twice.

Step 3 - Now take another mental inventory of how you feel.

You will notice that in just taking two conscious breaths you are experiencing a greater sense of inner connectedness and peace. This is Stress Reducing. You can do this exercise during the day as needed to get a little peace boost.

What just happened?

There is a connection between the state of the breath and the state of the mind. When the mind is agitated the breath is rapid and when the mind is calm the breath is calm. So when we consciously calm the breath, the mind becomes calmer, and when the mind becomes calmer the breath becomes calmer. This cycle of deeper and deeper levels of calmness is what we are attuning ourselves to when we meditate.

Overstimulation of the senses, through our many life experiences, causes agitation and stress to the mind. The calmer the mind, the easier it is to feel connected to the natural peace of the soul. This is why we talked earlier about simplifying our lives. The calmer our outward life, the easier it is to keep inwardly calm. Again, no matter what our lives look like on the outside, meditation is the most powerful and direct way to release stress and experience peace on the inside.

In Chapter Four we discussed the Full Yogic Breath and Deep Relaxation. Now we are going to add some more breathing and meditation techniques, all of which can be mixed and matched as you feel inclined. The key here is to remember that, just like exercise, you have to participate if you want to get the benefits. And the more you practice these techniques, the easier it will be to go deeper into their benefits.

The explanation of these techniques is in an extremely simplified form here, there is much more on this subject that would be helpful to you. I recommend that you read more about meditation and if possible you should attend a course in person.

I should mention one caution: When doing breathing exercises it is possible to get lightheaded, and in an extreme case, to faint. This is caused by forcing too much oxygen into the blood. If you ever feel lightheaded or tingly while doing the breathing exercises you should stop and rest until the feeling passes. Just like physical exercise, you should use common sense and build yourself up slowly.

Breathing Exercises

Calming Breath
Practice as described earlier in this chapter.

Full Yogic Breath
Practice as described in Chapter Four.

Equal Breathing
Inhale through the nose for 6 to 12 counts. Hold the breath for 6 to 12 counts. Exhale through the mouth for 6 to 12 counts. The key here is to have the inhalation, hold and exhalation all the same number. So it could be 6-6-6 or 8-8-8 or 12-12-12. If you get out of breath then lower the number of counts you are using. In the beginning repeat this only 3 times. Work up to 12 times.

Double Breathing with Tension

Just as we learned in the deep relaxation technique, inhale through the nose with a double breath – in, innnn - and exhale out through the mouth - out, ouuuut. As you inhale with the double breath, tense all the muscles in the body in a wave – low, medium, high – hold the tension and the breath for the count of three – and then relax the muscles in a wave – high, medium, low - as you exhale. This technique can be done standing, sitting or lying down. Do it 3 to 5 times. Again, if you feel dizzy at any time: stop. When you tense the muscles, check to make sure that all of the body is tensed. The axiom with this exercise is: Tense with will, relax and feel.

Sitting Meditation

Sit in a chair or cross-legged on the floor with a pillow. It is best if the back is straight and not leaning back, but if this is a problem then use a pillow to prop yourself up. If you try to meditate laying down you will probably fall asleep, which isn't bad, but it is not meditation.

Practice one or two of the breathing exercises as preparation for meditation.

With your eyes closed, begin your meditation practice by giving up control of the breath. Mentally watch the breath as it goes in and out of the body of its own accord. If your mind wanders, gently bring it back to watching the breath. If you find yourself controlling the breath, just relax and give up control again. The breath may be deep or shallow, it doesn't matter, just don't control it.

Now that you are watching the breath without controlling it you can add an additional way to engage the mind. As the breath comes in without your control mentally say "I am" and when the breath goes out of its own control say "Peace." So, as you watch the breath, you mentally repeat: I am, when the breath comes in, and, Peace, when the breath goes out.

Practice this for 5 to 20 minutes two or three times a day. It is best to practice for a shorter period of time regularly in the beginning and then over time to build up the duration.

Sitting in the Silence

After you finish your practice of a meditation technique it is very important to sit in the silence and enjoy the peace. This is actually an essential part of meditation.

Stress Solutions

Sitting in the inner silence is where you can steep your body, mind and spirit in a deep Stress Reducing state. Sit in the silence for as long as you can do so comfortably. When your mind says it is time to get moving, then try to carry this inwardly peaceful state with you into your activities.

Meditative Walking

While meditative walking isn't quite the same as meditation, you can use walking as a way to occupy the body enough to achieve a much calmer state of mind. We know that just walking in nature is calming. In the same way as taking those two conscious breaths worked earlier, when we walk consciously our perspective changes.

When possible, find the quietest place to walk with the freshest air. Walk at a comfortably slow pace. As you walk, mentally disconnect yourself from the world around you. Don't build a mental wall, but just relax and focus your attention on the breath, just as we did in the meditation exercise. Begin to watch the breath without controlling it. While you give up control of the breath, try to walk with a sense of freedom as well. The body knows what to do, mentally stand back from the body and focus on the breath. Now practice saying "I am" with the inhalation and "Peace" with the exhalation. Practice this for as long as you feel positively engaged.

When you are finished consciously watching the breath, then walk in the silence. Feel the inward peace that you have connected to. Then when you are ready, expand that peace to encompass your surroundings. Feel that you are walking in harmony with all of nature. Feel that you are one with the peace that sits at the center of all life.

Visualization

The mind is a powerful tool. You can take an inward Stress Reducing peace vacation any time you like. All you need to do is close your eyes and visualize yourself in an environment that feels good to you. You can mentally go to the beach, to the forest or to the top of a mountain. Just inwardly create a picture and the try to feel what that picture looks like. With practice you will be able to mentally transport yourself into a Stress Reducing state of mind. This is not the same as meditation, but it can be helpful.

If you have a well developed imagination this will be easy for you. If not, there are many audio CD's available that include a soft voice and soothing music. I encourage you to experiment with this. It is easy, fun and Stress Reducing.

Prayer

Many people don't realize that prayer has been tested in the laboratory with double blind studies. People who are prayed for heal faster and have better outcomes. Prayer is good for both the prayer and prayee. When we pray for others we are attuning ourselves to the universal power of love and goodness that is at the heart of all life. This in itself is Stress Reducing. We are also expanding the circle of our caring, which is Stress Reducing.

You don't need to pray for a specific outcome to help yourself and others. The universal healing power knows what is best to do when it arrives at the destination. Visualize yourself as a broadcasting station. Attune yourself inwardly through meditation to the universal healing presence and then broadcast that presence through your heart and out into the world and/or to the specific person or situation for which you are praying. If you want to, you can raise your hands and feel that the healing power is flowing through you and out your hands.

Prayer is not tied to any specific religion, though of course you can connect it to your religious practices if you want to. For those who consider this to be some sort of hocus pocus, I encourage you to experiment in the laboratory of your own life. Pray for someone or a situation and see what happens.

Just remember that selfish prayers inevitably lead to Stress Increasing results, selfless prayers lead to Stress Reducing peace of mind.

Meditation, Visualization and Prayer tips

• It is best if you are not full of food when you try to meditate.

• When you sit to meditate try to leave all thoughts of other activities behind, just put them mentally on the shelf and give your full attention to meditation.

• Don't judge the value of your prayer by your expectation of the results. Prayer for world peace is a great prayer, but don't assume your prayer failed to help in spite of the fact that the world isn't yet perfect. If you want to prove it works, start with something smaller than world peace or bringing a loved one back from the edge of death.

• For all of these practices, turn off the phone and retreat to the quietest place you can find. You can use earplugs and/or noise reduction headphones to help with noises.

•   A dark space is nice but not absolutely necessary. Remember, relaxed but focused attention is more important at first, and then duration.

•   Try to carry the feeling of peace that you experience during these exercises into the rest of your day.

•   You will find it helpful to practice meditation with others. Group effort is a powerful support. Try to find a group of likeminded meditators in your area.

"The peace of your soul awaits you
at the centre of your own being"
- Swami Kriyananda

Whatever forms of meditation you practice,
the most important point is to apply
mindfulness continuously, and make a
sustained effort. It is unrealistic to expect results
from meditation within a short period of time.
What is required is continuous sustained effort.
- Dalai Lama

The soul loves to meditate,
for in contact with Spirit lies its greatest joy.
If you experience mental resistance during
meditation, remember that reluctance to
meditate comes from the ego;
it doesn't belong to the soul."
- Paramhansa Yogananda

Chapter 9

Joy

It has been said many times, in many ways, that laughter is the best medicine. Have you ever wondered why this would be true? After all, having been to see medical doctors my fair share of times, not one of them have ever prescribed: Laugh three times a day and call me in the morning. I don't imagine they are giving others advice that they won't share with me. So, why would people say that laughter is the best medicine?

The Secret about Joy

The secret to this intuitively understood truth is that it isn't actually laughter that is the best medicine: Joy is the best medicine. Where can joy (happiness) be found? Within! How do we bring it out from within? We have been discussing a variety of ways, in this case, we are looking at laughter's potential for helping us to access joy that we already have within us.

So what is the big deal? Tell a joke, have a laugh, what else is there to say?

Stress Solutions

Well, the thing about laughter is that, like many other tools in life, it can be used to heal or it can be used to injure. When we tell stories and jokes that laugh *at* people, we are attuning ourselves to negative, Stress Increasing energy. When we laugh good naturedly *with* people, we are accessing positive joyful Stress Reducing energy. So it is the positive or negative direction of humor that determines the qualities of energy being accessed.

Laugh with Your Soul

Another aspect to this is how we laugh. What I mean is, are we laughing with calm, inwardly connected well meaning soul joy or are we out in our ego/personality whipping up our emotions into a frenzy which agitates the mind laughing? Restless laughing is agitating to the mind and is Stress Increasing due to the minds habit of balancing ups with downs. This is true with all activities that we enjoy. If we enjoy them with calmness they don't cause a corresponding let down. But if we enjoy life with strong emotions, we will always experience a balancing emotional letdown.

The key here is to learn to laugh with your soul and not your ego/personality. How do you do this? As you practice meditation regularly, you will begin to become aware of a calmer more balanced you that has been living inside your up and down personality. I am not talking about having a split personality! It is like a person who is wearing fancy clothes; are they the clothes or the person underneath? We think we are the ego/personality, which is how we appear on the outside, but we are actually the soul, which is the true person within. As we connect in ever deeper ways to our true self within we will experience more and more of our soul's natural state of equilibrium and joy. This joy isn't usually an outward need to laugh, though that could happen, but it is an upward flow of joyful wellbeing that just makes you feel happy. This is the "happiness is within" that is the most Stress Reducing and joy increasing.

Calmness, Positivity and Caring

In order to access this joy, practice meditation regularly. Calming the mind is essential. Maintain positive thoughts and live more to serve others than for your own fulfillment. One of the great secrets in life is to understand that genuinely caring about others leads to greater happiness. This doesn't mean just doing things for others, but giving freely, without thought of getting anything in return.

Having a positive mental attitude in life is also essential. If we spend our time with negative thoughts we will feel negative, it is just that simple. Negativity is Stress Increasing. At the same time, whipping up the mind into a hyperactive state of positivity is not the solution either. Again, whipping up the emotions in either a positive or negative direction is not beneficial - though I would say that if you are going to whip yourself up into a lather, doing it in a positive direction would be better than in a negative way!

Even-minded and Cheerful

What we really want to achieve is a mental state that is even-minded and cheerful most of the time. When we can face life's ups and downs with a positive, resilient, ready to smile and lend a helping hand attitude, we will experience less stress in life and more happiness. This even-minded state is a sign that our lives are in balance.

Increase Your Joy

While the solution to experiencing stress is on one hand to avoid and/or release stress, we don't often enough consider that increasing our joy level from within will make us happier and stronger so that life's challenges don't penetrate into our consciousness, thus instead of needing to reduce stress, we simple do not experience it.

The greatest solution to all of life's stresses is to learn how to access our spirit's natural inner peace, love and joy. When we do so, we will find that inspiration about how to proceed in life, in the best possible way, comes from that same inner place. In the next chapter we are going to talk specifically about how this works and ways to experiment with this in your own life.

Chapter 10

Solution Consciousness

When we are having a good day everything goes smoothly and we feel like we can handle anything. When we are having a bad day, it sometimes seems impossible to imagine how we will survive. According to the law of averages most of us will probably switch off from good days to bad days for the rest of our lives. When you think of it that way, life doesn't sound very appetizing. And to add spice to the situation, a number of lucky people will have good days for an extended period of time, and some unlucky folks will have a long string of bad days. Of course if you are on the lucky side; well what can you say? If you are on the unlucky side, life doesn't appear to be very fair. Come to think of it, doesn't this look a lot like gambling?

Do we really want to gamble with our happiness? Do we want to passively let the waves of life knock us about? Or do we want to do something about the situation? Of course if you have read this far, you must be in the "I am going to do something about this!" category.

But! I have another question. Why is it that we consider "bad" things in life bad?

Well in a general, we say that if something causes pain, it is bad. But is that really true? Isn't the pain of a sore tooth good, because it tells you to take care of a problem before it gets worse? Isn't the pain of the first time a child gets too close to a fire of long term benefit? The truth of life is that pleasure and pain have no good or bad value of their own. In fact some things that you consider pleasurable might be painful to someone else. Clearly this is true with different kinds of foods. Even as a young boy I instinctively knew that you could put as much chocolate on an ant as you want, I still wasn't going to eat it. And chocolate covered ants are nothing compared to the variety of bugs and strange concoctions that people around the world have learned to enjoy.

It is what we do with all of our life experiences that will determine in the long run if an experience is beneficial or not beneficial, Stress Reducing or Stress Increasing. That which is helpful in one person's life might be a hindrance in another person's life. So it is more practical if we don't put the label of good or bad on our life experiences and just face them with the even-mindedness that we discussed in the last chapter.

When we choose to face life with even-minded cheerfulness, which we have strengthened through meditation and a positive approach to life, we will have built the foundation upon which we can live in solution consciousness - Stress Reducing - instead of problem consciousness - Stress Increasing.

As we have discussed, life is what we make of it. No matter how smooth or how rough the road ahead looks, our attitude will make all of the difference. When we look at life challenges with a negative attitude we see nothing but problems. When we approach life with a positive attitude we see only opportunities. This is so important, that I will say it again: Happiness in life is not an issue of what happens; it is a choice about how we react to what happens. When we choose to live in solution consciousness we will find that even a bumpy road can be smoothed out through our inner attunement to happiness and life's ever present positive potential. When we choose to live in problem consciousness we reap the unhappiness that results from that choice.

Solution consciousness is not just a positive attitude that we paste on the surface of our personality, but it is the active process of our inner connection to wellbeing and inspiration from within. When the mind is calm and the spirit is open, we will find that life is our friend. This doesn't mean that everyday will be a picnic and we won't have challenges, but it does mean that we will have access to solutions, inner strength and peace of mind to face those challenges. Through the practice of everything that we have been talking about you will experience an inner understanding and harmony that is powerfully Stress Reducing and challenge solving.

We are now going to look at some examples of Problem Consciousness versus Solution Consciousness. Since most of us are mixtures of the two, these examples may seem extreme, but for our purposes these extremes will help us to understand clearly the differences in these two approaches to life. As we look at these scenarios, honestly evaluate which way your mind's inclination would turn if you were in this situation.

Fired from Job

Problem Consciousness: Why me? Those xxxx xxxx idiots, they should fire themselves! I am going to get them! There goes my savings! I need a drink!

Solution Consciousness: Wow, a vacation! This would be a great time to make that career switch that I was thinking about. I am sure glad I have some savings!

Evaluation: Problem Consciousness loves to blame others and dwell on negative things like revenge and drinking away one's problems: none of these lead to an improvement of the situation, but increases the negative potential. Solution Consciousness immediately finds humor and/or positive potentials in the situation. They both had savings: one saw a negative view, the other a positive view.

Arguing with Spouse

Problem Consciousness: Why do you always do that? It is not my fault! Stop nagging me! Why do we have to go over this again and again, it's always the same! You don't know what you are talking about! To XXXX with you! I need a drink!

Solution Consciousness: I am sorry I have been grumpy lately, I have been feeling stressed, can I have a hug? Can you please explain your point of view again? I want to listen more carefully. I am sorry I haven't been more sensitive to your needs, let's talk. It seems like we have been arguing more lately, what do you say we take an argument vacation? We seem to be at an impasse here, what do you say we go talk with a friend/counselor?

Evaluation: Again, Problem Consciousness equals the blame game and negative expressions that lead to more stress and negativity; virtually guaranteeing no positive outcome. In Solution Consciousness we can accept blame and ask for forgiveness. Offer solutions without pointing the finger at others. We also realize that there is a time to ask for help from our spouse, friends and/or counselors.

Poor Communication with Children

Problem Consciousness: You guys are driving me crazy, go to your room! If you guys don't quiet down I am going to come in there!

Solution Consciousness: Hey kids, come here, let's talk. Why are you guys all excited? Do you need something to do? I was thinking we could go for a bike ride, what do you think? Do you want to help me make dinner?

Evaluation: In this situation Problem Consciousness tried to avoid the situation by getting rid of it with a one way communication of punishment and a threat. Solution Consciousness sought out real two way communication and ways to redirect the children's energy into positive directions. The offer of a bike ride also said: I like/love you and want to spend time with you.

Money Stress

Problem Consciousness: Why doesn't the government fix this economy? Why is this happening to me? This is just great, I can't catch a break! I need a drink!

Solution Consciousness: I am feeling stressed by this situation, I think I will go meditate. I am going to sit down and see where I can economize my expenditures. I wonder if there is a way I could make some extra money with my hobby?

Evaluation: As you probably anticipated, Problem

Stress Solutions

Consciousness is still busy blaming others, stewing in his own juices and looking to drink some more special juice as a means of escape. Solution Consciousness is taking the time to feel peace in a challenging time. Then practical steps are taken to explore possible Stress Reducing solutions.

Death in the Family

Problem Consciousness: Uncontrolled grief. Having negative thoughts about the deceased. Over concern about a possible inheritance. Poor attitude toward friends of the deceased that you don't like.

Solution Consciousness: Grief that recognizes death as a part of life and is heartfelt while not being additionally stress producing. Positive prayer for the wellbeing of the deceased and all grievers. More concerned about others than yourself.

Evaluation: It is Stress Reducing to be more concerned about others than yourself. And of course, blaming the dead for anything is pretty pointless, while at the same time being Stress Increasing. When we let our emotions get out of control, even if the basis of those emotions is positive, we actually create stress and allow negative energy to pollute a positive feeling. While it is appropriate to be concerned about the transition of a person's estate, it is Stress Increasing to have selfish thoughts.

Health Challenge

Problem Consciousness: Why me? I can't believe this is happening! Anger. Just let me die!

Solution Consciousness: Calm acceptance of current circumstances and a positive attitude toward helping

Solution Consciousness

to make things better. Having concern about the concern of others. Smiling in the face of adversity.

Evaluation: Denial, blame, anger, and self-pity are all pathways to greater stress and dark feelings. No matter what happens in life, when we choose to smile and do our best, we will bring a positive potential to even the most difficult circumstances.

Life is Disappointing

Problem Consciousness: They have gotten me again. This world is hell. I need a drink/drugs. Everyone is against me. This is all their fault! I have been treated unfairly. I may as well give up. What's the point?

Solution Consciousness: Things have been rough lately, but I am not going to give up. I noticed that Mrs. Jones needs her lawn mowed; I think I will go offer to help. I think I will spend some time in prayer, seeking guidance about how to move my life in a better direction.

Evaluation: Negative thoughts beget negative feelings which beget negative experiences. The circle of negative consciousness is self fulfilling. It doesn't take all that much to turn a dark day into a positive day. Just offer to help someone with their problems and your problems will get smaller. The best solution for hopelessness is to feel positive energies flowing through your life. That means putting your energy into giving and letting the receiving take care of itself. And of course, spend time with the source of life itself, unburden your heart, and humbly ask for guidance. This will certainly be Stress Reducing and you may find that God/Nature/the Universe will respond!

As we can see, Problem Consciousness doesn't help. It not only doesn't solve problems, it increases the

81

chances that there will be more problems: thus leading to Stress Increasing results. On the other hand, Solution Consciousness lessens the sting of problems right away and leads to long term beneficial solutions. This is practical in terms of resolving challenges and Stress Reducing at the same time.

Now it is up to you.

The school of hard knocks is where we are tested in life. Unfortunately, most of us didn't receive a complete course in "How to live without stress" training while we were growing up. But now you have no excuse. We have reviewed a number of powerful ways to Reduce Stress and avoid or at least diminish Stress Increasing influences.

When a person becomes physically fit, they can handle a wide variety of exercises with little stress. When we become fit in body, mind and spirit, there are few life challenges that can stress us. And when we do feel stressed, we will have the tools and experience to step up to the challenge with confidence. This type of self-confidence is not bluster, but strength earned through the positive application of the principles we have been discussing.

The most central solution to stress is our inner connection to the source of wellbeing and understanding within us. When we bring inner balance to our lives, we will experience the strength and flexibility that it takes to dance through life with our own unique style and a smile.

I wish you success in life's greatest challenge, the exploration of your own higher self. And I hope these ideas will bring you freedom from stress and a greater awareness of your soul's nature as love, peace and joy.

More books
by Lawrence Vijay Girard
(Nayaswami Vijay)

Way of the Positive Flow

Meditation:
The Science and Art of Stillness

Flowing in the Workplace:
A Guide to Personal and Professional Success

Positive Flow Parenting

Doorway to a New Lifetime:
Childbirth from a Spiritual View

The Journey of Discipleship
Book 1 - Traveling with Swamiji

The Adventures of Harry Fruitgarden Series
Book #1 - What's it All About?
Book #2 - Who Would Have Guessed?

Ask us about
Positive Flow Seminars
with Lawrence Vijay Girard

---

www.FruitgardenPublishing.com

www.ingramcontent.com/pod-product-compliance
Lightning Source LLC
Chambersburg PA
CBHW071017040426
42443CB00007B/815